CW00821720

Poems of Substance

For an Uncertain World

John Deed

Published by John Deed, Thriplow, England

www.flyingpigments.co.uk

ISBN 978-1-8382787-4-8
Text and image copyright © John Deed, 2024

With thanks to www.freepik.com for some of the illustrations.

Front cover by John Deed Photography
www.johndeed.co.uk

To My Family

Who provide the safety net under the fledgling
flying hopes of inspiration

Still in memory of Cal

Index

Part 1. Chameleon Called Love

Part 2. Nostalgia and Nostradamus

Part 3. Black Dogs & White Cats

Part 4. Existence and Non-Existence

Introduction

Since my first book of poetry ("Elemental Poems. Of Being. Of the Mind. Of the Heart."), published in the Covid times of 2021, it seems a crazy world has got crazier, with the peaks and troughs of hope and despair getting ever more amplified.

Social inequality is wider, our so-called leaders have become more extreme, the dialogue on media platforms has become angrier and the lines between truth and untruth seem ever more blurred. Institutions and infrastructures don't seem fit for purpose but we seem powerless to fix them. It feels like a relentless march to somewhere we know isn't good.

But, in the face of this we must try and retain hope that things will be different and will change. Little acts of kindness remind us that, on a local level at least, love and happiness can be found and that with enough of these we may make a better whole. And that although meaning and understanding might not be found in a silicon chip, it can be found in the material from whence the silicon came, namely one of Blake's grains of sand.

And so, this second book explores some of the same themes and I make no apology for this, but with new light and perspective. The fickle word of love, the nature of existing on our tiny planet, the very different sides of humanity and issues of the mind. Dealing with the very big and very small, and also that middle ground morass where life is played out. All things which occupy my thought process, and on which I have different views, depending on my mood and outlook.

I hope you will enjoy these poems and they will at once stimulate and resonate. Comfort and challenge. Awaken and calm.

Part 1.

Chameleon Called Love

Mercurial Love

Love loves

Love hurts

Love pleases

Love pains

Love burns

Love cools

Love shines

Love rains.

Love soars

Love glides

Love ebbs

Love flows

Love swims

Love dives

Love's blind

Love knows.

Love runs

Love walks

Love laughs

Love cries

Love breathes

Love whispers

Love shouts

Love sighs.

4

Love sees

Love hears

Love frowns

Love smiles

Love cuts

Love mends

Love explains

Love beguiles.

Love is all these things and more

Love is love and love is all

Smile

Hello. Welcome back

I haven't seen you in a while

The sum of all that's happiness

Your easy loving smile

- - - - - - - - - - - - - - - - - - -

I Love You

"I love you" she said

Those three words

Cupid's triumvirate

Rolled off her tongue

And gathered speed

Unstoppable momentum

Rolling out of control

Down the road of fate

An indelible mark

On time itself

Where

No thought

No action

Absolutely nothing

Would

Be the same

Mean the same

Feel the same

Ever

Again

You'll Be Around Forever (Won't You?)

You've been around forever
Since time began for me
Gentle, warm, a living rock
When I am all at sea

Through misty dreams and rocky roads
Arms always open wide
Each step made on my journey
Your presence by my side

Stars they shine so far above
The sun lights up the day
More constant still is your love
That conquers come what may

So simple and so easy
Your selfless, fearless mind
Ask for nothing in return
Each action made so kind

No lectures or instruction
Just being pure and true
No acting or high drama
You do, just do, you do

If we could all be half as good
And be so half the time
What a place this world would be
A paradise sublime

Way beyond life's finite grains
That glide from hence to past
You'll be around forever (won't you?)
Love that til time's end will last

I Am Life

I am life
I am hope
I am love
Magic and stardust
From the heavens above
An impossible dream
A miraculous scheme
Hatched in a womb dark and warm
I know how to grow
I know how to form
Into tangible body
And ethereal soul

Silent gathering of atoms
Whose destiny through time is now
An elaborate ritual
Of order and sequence
An invisible code
Written only for me
Nourished by a solitary cord
Tethered to all mothers before
And yet despite this wonder
I know nothing of your world
The world of light and air
I am not schooled
I am not learned
My rooms for knowledge
Yet empty and bare
But I will know how to laugh
And cry
And feel
And fear
I will know how to see
I will know how to hear
So please take care
Of what you show and tell me
What you think or say

What you do or don't
Each action or reaction
That will add or take away
From this impressionable being
Born in one finite moment
To this great infinite universe
That to most will be
Just an ordinary day
But for me
It will be *my* day
My time
And I will shine
With unsung birds and bees
Bugs and beasts
And plants and trees
We will enter the world
Partners united
To ensure the circle of life goes on
But what life will it be?
May those early years be blessed
With legs that run and run
A heart that beats
With joy and fun

And when the days of innocence are done

May I be fair

May I be wise

May I be kind

May there be true love that I find

May I have strength and will

From an uncluttered mind

To play my part as best I can

To hold the baton passed to my hand

To do that which is left undone

To right wrongs that have caused pain

To bring accord where there's strife

To pay attention to that in neglect

To have the time to reflect

Let me be love

Let me be hope

Let me be life

Light and Shade

You run deep like the river
Yet flow light like the stream
You know that life's for living
But that some things aren't as they seem

You're easy and you're complex
Rich in character like fine wine
A hidden gem so precious
Brightest diamond in the mine

At once fun and friendly
Yet dependable, loyal and true
Taking your time to decide
Taking your time to make a move

Subtle blend of light and shade
A genial contradiction
Always knowing right from wrong
Always telling fact from fiction

Original curvy thinker
With a child's inquisitive mind
A wonder for the world around you
Yet seeing truth straight down the line

You're the friend to depend on
You're the friend to share good times
You know we're just dust and water
But that water tastes better as wine

And if I was in a hard place
I know I could count on you
Right by my side whatever
Determined to help me get through

So don't ever change your ways
Keep to the furrow you're ploughing
And the sun will surely shine
On all the goodness you're growing

- - - - - - - - - - - - - - - - - - - -

Bedsit Lovers

Daily letters
Sealed with a kiss
Time and distance are meaningless
Coins for weekday phone box calls
A few minutes to express

13

Week's now over
The train connects
Once more coupled arm in arm
Steel City, Snake Pass, Piccadilly
Humming "railway carriage charm"

A single room
A single bed
A single bar electric fire
Ancient clothes horse by the window
Gentle breeze for a drier

Picture hook holes
Brown frame outlines
Of family photos that once hung
On off-white anaglypta walls
Tell of bygone days unsung

A half warm hob
To heat the food
Two knives, two forks, two cups, two bowls
Two young hearts that beat as one
From two connected souls

Cheap red wine box
Take-away tins
Tupperware boxes with no covers
Hissing cassette tape music
To serenade the lovers

Warm skin on skin
And lips on lips
Aphrodite's rose unfurled
Cotton candy sheets and pillows
Wrapped up in their world

Love was love
In those dreamy times
The same as love is love today
All the rest is immaterial
There's nothing more to say

Southern Honey

Got an old felt fedora set on straight

And calf skin boots for walking interstate

On the road again, like Smokestack Sam

Leaving the city limits of Selma, Alabam

Dirty swamp music playin' loud in my heart

Old lagoon tunes with no end and no start

Headin' down south to God knows where

Lookin' for a life in the easy chair

Hopin' to spend some quality time

With that sweet Southern honey who's mine, all mine

Straw blonde hair and a heart of gold

She's much too hot for the Devil to hold

I'll stay a few days or maybe a week

Long enough anyhow to end my losin' streak

And if all goes well and her heartstrings sing

Maybe she'll accept this pawned diamond ring

Or maybe she won't and I'll look like a fool

A Kerouac clown unlearned and unschooled

Scarlett O'Hara

She goes by the name of Scarlett O'Hara

And her heart's somewhere deep

In Guadalajara

You can probably find her

In the dive bars and whisky joints

Where all the men think they own her

But nobody's ever taken time to show her

What love is

And what she really needs

But nonetheless

I'll always respect her

Her fortune telling ways

And her travelling eyes

But I'll never expect her

To give me a second thought

Though she's lost like me

And she doesn't seem to see

That love can't be bought

It must be free

But when I'm drinking

And my mind starts thinking

Of her skin so dark and brown

Her swaying hips

Her hypnotic dance
I'm going drive to the heart
Of that beat up town
And gamble my last coin
On the roulette wheel of chance

Purple Haze

I read your thoughts through a purple haze
Sorry I misunderstood your holy ways
Sorry I showed you a promised land
And then I walked away

Shifting Sands

I wrote poetry in the sand for you
Painted pictures in the river
Bared my soul in the wind
But like your love
That slipped through my fingers
Nothing but memory remains

There's No Limit to Love

All that's material is finite
But there's no limit to love
If you open your eyes
And make a small start
Loving your neighbours
Will open your heart
Then brothers and sisters
Whether family or not
Love will blossom and grow
You'll never run short
All that you know
All that you can't
The benefit of doubt
Is love's given a chance
And love is for life
Love is for giving
The secret ingredient
The meaning of living
You cannot divide it
Or hide it or dim it
The infinite well
Of love has no limit

Beacon

Constant, dazzling

Bright white beacon

Of lighthouse hopes

Heart-warming uplifter

To those who travel

With spinning compass

Through stair rod rain

Lashed by despair

And blown off course

By dark and threatening forces

But standing steadfast

On terra firma

At the headland of life's rocky bay

You shine for me

When I am alone

Always and come what may

Honeysuckle Dreams

Honeysuckle dreams

Heaven's scent

Beguiles this busy bee

There's something enchanting about you

That you were always meant

Sweetest honey

Just for me

I Promise

I promise you I'll be here

Whatever the future brings

Loving you the best I can

Until the last song bird sings

Half-Life of Hurt

Their love was like

Nuclear fusion

But they were under

No illusion

That even the brightest stars implode

And collapse into a void

Somewhere down the road
When warm memories begin to fade
And the happy tunes have all been played
And a tide of gloom
Grows ever deeper
Engulfing the dreams
Of the heavy sleeper
Where darkness starts to outlive the light
When the legs are heavy
And the heart won't fight
Transition to an endless night
The half-life of hurt is a long, long time

Simply Love

Life was so much simpler
No shiny gadgets to rule our lives
Just a coin into the phone box
And 5 minutes to say I love you
And hear that you loved me too
Then time to think and ponder
On passion so far apart
Yet so visceral and real
Our loving cup renewed once more
To sustain the way we'd feel

Sedimentary Thoughts

The backbone of her spirit was bowed
Burdened by unexpressed feelings
Words unsaid
And unspoken thoughts
Broken promises
And unrequited love
Buried by the weight of days
That accumulate slowly with time
Layer upon layer upon layer
Like sediment laid down
Across the seasons
Imperceptibly built up
To a dense, impervious mass
Hiding fossils of resentment and remorse
Remnants of a life unlived

The Wire

I've taken it all
Right down to the wire
To stop me loving you
It's like using snow to fight fire

The draw of your love
Upon my poor soul
Fatal attraction
Mesmeric magnet, North to South pole

No matter how hard
I pull on the reins
I can't stop this blood
From running red hot through my veins

I've done what I can
I broke all the rules
To be by your side
Following a light shined for fools

But what do I care
What harm can it do
I'm hopelessly bound
Forever and ever, only to you

- - - - - - - - - - - - - - - - - - - -

I Hope

I hope you'll always find joy in simple things
Whatever chance and choice may bring
And your heart beats with love and innocence
Now and always from this day hence

- - - - - - - - - - - - - - - - - - - -

Seasoned Oak

My love is like the seasoned oak
Fine grained and strong it will not bend
Being there for you and with you
In the silence of the universe
Forever in your presence, love
Sweet truth and sweet end

I will always stand right by you
And I will always hold your hand
I will always lay beside you
Till the lights are dimmed and others gone
When we are once more meadow dew
And holy grains of sand

Right Here, Right Now

The universe of galaxies
Of comets, planets and stars
Of mountains, oceans, rivers and canyons
Of birds and bees and flowers and trees
These are of no concern to me
I see nor feel for one of them

Because right here, right now
You are my everything
The centre of all that is my world

I Don't Suppose We Ever Will

Another day, another night
Time's marching like it never did before
In the wastelands of my mind
There's another hour to kill
What would it take to make it our finest?
I don't suppose we ever will

Slipping slowly through my fingers
Like the golden sands from some far off shore
Paths crossing, never aligning
But I'll keep waiting until
Our stars align in the jet-black sky
I don't suppose they ever will

So many dreams evaporate
Floating up to make someone else's cloud
The rocky road is crumbling
So many holes yet to fill
We could yet make it the perfect highway
I don't suppose we ever will

Sleep walking to the horizon
Grazing in the lowlands and the valleys
Can't hear the alarm bells ringing
I'm still stuck down at the foot of the hill
I'd have loved us to meet on the mountain
I don't suppose we ever will

No Carpe Diem

With furrowed brow
And harrowed skin
Myopic thoughts concealing
A cataract heart within
Days roll by
And years pile up
He succumbs to the march of time
The numbness of familiarity
Same tune, same words, same rhyme
The complacency of companionship
His is not a happy place
No carpe diem here
Just opportunity gone to waste
Retreated from the laughter lines
He exists only in shadows
And never makes the most
A man no more
An apparition
A lifeless living ghost

Fly

Fly my pretty thing, fly

Open your wings

And touch the sky

Your delight is my delight

This day and forever

We are as one

Still together

Bound by love's infinity

And yet eternally untethered

Two unbreakable links

In a weightless chain

You are you

And you are free

And I stand content

Like a faithful falconer

Feeling your pleasure

As you glide and soar

And when you're ready to return

I'll offer up an outstretched arm

And you'll come back to me

Eye of the Storm

I gaze into the infinity of your eyes
I see storm clouds and shipwrecks
And a thousand alibis

I see dense dark forests and wild black oceans
I see the seven of swords
And a chalice of potions

I see howling winds and sideways driving rain
I see a longing for love
But acceptance of pain

And at the epicentre a mysterious hole
To another world beyond
A gateway to your soul

Gone Fishing

He decided to go fishing
To cast his net among the glistening shoals
And see if he could get some
But he ignored the warnings
That as well as many fine fish in the sea
There's a lot of flotsam and jetsam

Adonis

His pylon spine

Carried limbs of power

He stood foursquare

Like the Eiffel tower

Cannonball guns

Pecs like slabs

Calfs like rocks

And granite abs

Vice like hands

Thighs like trees

But just a little dose

Of Aphrodite's love

Brought him crashing to his knees

Satellite Dreams

Your satellite love goes round and round

Silently crossing the sky

On dark and lonely black hole nights

I see shooting stars and meteorites

As I watch the heavens roll by

Sardine Lives

Side by side

All hemmed in

Sardine lives

Where no-one wins

Petty words

Withering looks

He watches TV

While she cooks

The sorry state

Of lives impaired

No warmth or love

No duties shared

"What *are* you doing?"

Never asking *how*

Not the words

Of wedding vows

Expunged dreams

Of harmony

Ground out existence

Of attritional proximity

Cusp of Change

To everything there's a season
And my season here is done
Everything for a reason
It's time for me to run

- - - - - - - - - - - - - - - - - - -

Holy One

Your sunshine smile
And moonbeam eyes
Your starlit heart
Can tell no lies
You are the only one
You are the holy one
Indivisible
Love's singularity sublime

- - - - - - - - - - - - - - - - - - -

I'm Sorry

I'm sorry for any hurt
I'm sorry for any pain
I'm sorry for so much time
That was less than perfect
In the long dark days of rain

- - - - - - - - - - - - - - - - - - -

Keep the Child Safe Within You

Wherever life may take you
Wherever you should go
Whatever they might tell you
Whatever you come to know
Whatever way the wind blows
Whether it's rain or shine
Whatever you are feeling
Whether it's rough or fine
Whatever doors you find open
Whatever gates stay shut
Whether you sleep in a mansion
Whether you rest in a shepherd's hut
Wherever paths may lead you
Whatever bridges you have built
Whether crowns are placed upon your head
Whether they burden you with guilt
Whatever luck may throw your way
Whatever you choose to do
Leave a space for innocence
And keep the child safe within you

- - - - - - - - - - - - - - - - - - - -

Yours Sincerely

Forever yours
With fond regards
Words of lovers
Words of bards
Heaven sent
With a loving kiss
Avec bisous
It's you I miss
Mi amor
And mon ami
I'm for you
And you're for me
Lovesick heart
My soul enfeebling
The pain of love
Meine kleiner liebling
Je t'embrasse
Or if you prefer
Je t'aime toujours
Mon petit coeur
Whatever the words
I love you dearly
Now and always
I'm yours, sincerely

End of Part 1

Part 2.

Nostalgia and Nostradamus

The Living Room

Open coal fireplace

Brass bucket and tongs

Marble mantlepiece

Where family snaps belong

Tea cup rings

On the occasional table

Record precious moments

Of time taken when able

Important papers

In the hinged leather stool

Near the Bakelite phone

Which no-one calls

Functional wall clock

Silent, no chimes

Time stood still

At ten past nine

Thick velvet drapes

Opaque net curtains

Window pane cataracts

With years of dirt on

Behind the shade

Of the standard lamp

A patch of mould

From rising damp

Maroon flock wallpaper

Past sensuous feeling

Dried edges lifting

Corners all peeling

Dark wooden dresser

Not too ornate

With Jubilee jugs

And Coronation plates

Empty decanter

Silver tray tarnished

Cribbage box

With jaundiced varnish

Liqueurs and sherries

Half drunk, put away

Expectantly stored

For the next special day

Other people's news

In the newspaper rack

Real milestones of time

In holiday nick-nacks

Soft, shabby sofa

Beige and brown

Cushions frayed

Springs sagging down

Faded florals

Hint at former glories

Rich repository

Of life's small stories

Red wine stains

And buttons missing

Creaky frame

From too much kissing

Gullies and ginnels

Time capsule den

Of biscuit crumbs

And missing pens

Threadbare arms

A place to pause

Worn out relief

From daily chores

Fossilised imprints

In the ancient Wilton

Deep pile foundations

A world was built on

It's hard to see

In the gas-light gloom

But there was once much living

In this living room

Emperor's New Clothes

The black brick mill chimney memories

Of hollowed out northern towns

Still reverberate to bygone sounds

The thumping drum and trumpet

Of the works brass band

Of cast iron machines

Worked by hard skin hands

Where hissing steam

And straining voices

Are echoes of the past

The fabric of society

Bedevilled tombs of notoriety

Are resurrected in another land now

Where labour's cheap as microchips

Where loose laws and tight lips

Have taken up the slack

And I wonder if in turn one day

They too will fall silent

Replaced by what?

God knows!

I can't imagine

No matter how hard I try

Surely not the great AI!

Who will make the emperor's clothes?

The Old Bakery

Early to rise
At half past three
But first things first
A pot of tea
Metal kettle
Set on the hob
Mind turns once more
To tins and cobs
Whilst water fresh
Warms to a boil
The baker starts
His daily toil
Stiff joints, cold limbs
Unearthly hour
Routine habits
Provide the power
Light the ovens
To light the soul
A hundredweight
Of British coal
Hewn by hand
In Yorkshire's seams

Fuel to make *his* fuel
For factory teams
And office workers
On morning trains
Fuel to inspire
Creative brains
Bustling children
Square sandwich packs
And busy mums'
Quick lunchtime snacks
The produce of
The bakery
Economic
Prosperity
This brief muse done
It's back to tasks
What comes next
No need to ask
His mug now filled
With inky brew
He tweaks and trims
The chimney flue
Dark art of fire
Sixth sense and tricks
To fully heat

The oven's bricks

Time to dress this

Saintly patron

In tall white hat

And canvas apron

His strong arms lift

The flour sacks filled

With finest grains

Locally milled

From native wheat

Precisely ground

By granite stones

The wind turned round

The baker takes

A gulp of tea

Brand-new day, but

Same recipe

Precise amounts

Salt, sugar, fat

Mixed by the man

In the magic hat

His creation

A doughy beast

Given its life

By fertile yeast

Pummelled, kneaded

Time honoured moves

The pregnant loaves

Are left to prove

Knock back, repeat

Just like before

Now ready for

The oven door

Laid out on trays

Baked just for us

They rise again

Like Lazarus

Light white centre

Encased in gold

A visual feast

Sight to behold

It's judgement time

To meet their maker

Master craftsman

The village baker

He breaks a loaf

Lifts to his nose

Complex bouquet

It's cooked *just so*

Amen, thanks be

They've passed the test

Now time to pack

And stack the rest

Some for the shop

Some for the van

Predestined name

Upon each one

As the pale dawn

Lights nascent skies

Mere mortals rouse

With sleepy eyes

Preparing for

The day ahead

Give them this day

Their daily bread

Village Cricket

She dreams, she dreams

Of men in white

The first eleven

On summer nights

Cable knits

And cotton flannels

Synthetic shirts

With mesh sweat panels

She dreams, she dreams

Of men in white

Sponsors' logos

Coloured bright

Noble sport

In the fairest land

Opening bat

Wood in hand

She dreams, she dreams

Of men in white

Swinging left

Or swinging right

Grass so green

And balmy weather

Pleasuring sound of

Willow on leather

She dreams, she dreams

Of men in white

Box inserted

Helmet tight

One by one

Imagined lovers

Creaming shots

Through the covers

She dreams, she dreams

Of men in white

Men of spirit

Men of fight

Close knit team

Hands to the pump

Taking guard

On middle stump

She dreams, she dreams

Of men in white

Like a moth

Drawn to the light

Of the bowlers

She likes them slow

Finger spinners

She'd like to know

She dreams, she dreams

Of men in white

Wistful wonder

Of what might

Dawn approaches

Restless sighs

Polished balls

On muscled thighs

She wakes, she wakes

No men in white

Lathered, fretful

End of night

Later on

Thoughts well kept

None will know

Just how she slept

And at the ground

Weak in the knee

She brings her gift

The cricketer's tea

They dream, they dream

Of first-class fare

A royal feast

Laid out to share

Knowing not of

Reciprocal love

Her Victoria sponges

From Heaven above

They dream, they dream

Of first-class fare

Paper plates

And doilies square

Caring not

How they should bowl

Thinking only of

The sausage rolls

They dream, they dream

Of first-class fare

Moist frangipane

Tarts topped with pear

At the crease

Chasing two five two

She puts the Assam

On to brew

They dream, they dream

Of first-class fare

Trays of plenty made

With love and care

Minds on buns not runs

Hoping not to linger

Playing reckless shots

To yield the umpire's finger

They dream, they dream

Of first-class fare

Thick sandwich filled

With beef so rare

Last man, no stroke, leg before

All out for sixty-three

But frankly no one gives a fig

As it means an early tea

Card Players

It's around one o'clock
At the Moulin café
The sun beats down from above
Weary church bells chime
Flat notes out of time
And like time
Their sound drifts away

Two expressionless men
At once close and aloof
Hats keep their hands in the shade
Steely eyes that squint
Cede no clue or hint
Just hiding
Three cards and the truth

Distant lavender fields
Hazy mauve to the eye
Tin tables laid out for lunch
A feeling of peace
Cloudy glass of anise
Just watching
The world passing by

And fresh crusty baguettes
Made by Madame Bertrand
Dipped in thick gold olive oil
Whilst on the next seat
A man has moules frites
And a glass
Of Sauvignon Blanc

Thick ochre walls dappled
By the leafy plane trees
Listen to the daily tales
The old metal sign
For Luberon wine
Swings gently
In the occasional breeze

Peeling shutters held fast
With their cast iron ties
Let light touch the scene within
A bar steeped in stories
Tragedies and glories
A witness
To thousands of lives

But at the table outside
The card players arise
Long handshake and warm embrace
Holistic, habitual
Intimate ritual
While above
A black raven cries

Human Roulette

Some people got monsoon rains
Some got fertile land
Some people got liquid gold
Some got desert sand
Some people got lush green forests
Some got guns and saws
Some people got peace and love
Some got hate and wars
Some people got all they wanted
Some got nothing at all
Some people got to mountain tops

Some were born to fall

It's dog eat dog and man eat man

The laws of the jungle and roulette

Can we rise above and work together?

I wouldn't want to bet

- - - - - - - - - - - - - - - - - - - -

Keys to Power

They say the pen

Is mightier than the sword

But not as mighty

As the plastic keyboard

Letters of love

And letters of hate

One on one

Or nation states

Sticks and stones

Never broke your bones

But words will

Always hurt you

Maybe black

Or maybe white

Honest as day

Or fly by night

Gospel truth
Or fake preacher
Deadly prose
Will instantly reach you

No conversation
Face to face
Memes and handles
No name to trace

Hit the return
In a blink
No time to pause
No time to think

Twenty-six letters
All laid out
Yours to choose
Sing or shout

Healing words
Or retribution
Logged forever
Your contribution

Heard at least
You've got a voice
And with it comes
A conscious choice

We all travel
Down different roads
Live our lives
By different codes

Sitting naked
Or combat dressed
Search for peace
Or provoke unrest

See you later
Soon be home
Or see you later
We've sent the drone

24/7

Roger's in the cockpit

Pulling on the joystick

But don't dive too low

You might have a little mishap

Next thing you know

Kathy's at the clinic

Talking high-flying clap-trap

Shadow in the shade

He's way down deep in Hades

The billion-dollar soccer star

Is busy making passes

And goes to tackle

The ladies in Mercedes

At the step aerobics classes

Very chic! Very hip!

Chloe's cooked her chilli dip

In Oxford town

Where Don, the oily roister doister

Smorgasbord and gown

Opens his throat

To slip down an oyster in the cloister

Maxim, max it, mach two
Twenty four seven go!
Chemical cocktails
Party with the glitterati
There's just no time to fail
Must get on with the show
Keep calm with zen and karate

Seriously no joke
Buy now before it's broke
Guilty consumption junkie
Talks of helping the poor
So when feeling hungry
For a take-away drove
His Ferrari to Harare

You clock-in, clock-out
To get heard you need to shout
Forget more than you know
While o'er the hills and far away
Kid in the ghetto
Has been crying out
Mama, please, *please* get a break today

- - - - - - - - - - - - - - - - - - - -

Press Here

He's here!

He's all around!

Whatever you're doing

You'll surely be found

He's come from the sun

He's come from the stars

He's lurking in bedrooms

He's loitering in bars

You know you've got secrets

Don't believe you'll get caught?

Don't believe in his power?

Don't believe you'll be bought?

Someone's been bugging you

Got under your skin

Drinking your blood

The enemy within

Honeypots and boobytraps

Snares, tricks and mines

Listening for whispers

And tell-tale signs

World without purpose

Where anything goes

Liberty's a shackle

Because everyone knows

Some people regret

The times in decline

They're sitting and waiting

For some kind of sign

But they fail to see

The future is here

That judgement day's daily

You can read it so clear

Don't you think it is strange?

Don't you think that it's odd?

Ethereal medium

New deity, new God

Every word for the record

Indelibly there

For ever and ever

Amen, say your prayers

Trust Yourself

Trust your own ears

Trust your own eyes

To tell the difference

Between truth and lies

Human Kind

You painted a cross on my door
You stitched a star on my jacket breast
You tattooed a number on my arm
You carved your initials in my chest

You were the master of the moment
Who put the branding iron to my face
A hideous coward of the third degree
King of the inhuman race

Difference is a double edge sword
For your lies and hate and fear
But mark my words, your cards are marked
Your judgement's drawing near

And when it does I will rejoice
You'll come to regret your birth
And all the time you spent doing wrong
To the innocent of the earth

For I am human kind
Stronger than the stars above
Where differences are unbreakably bound
By the common thread of love

Unknown Soldier

Listen to the bell

It tolls for each one

Another oak fallen

Another life undone

The filth of war

For one barely a man

Defending freedoms

In an occupied land

I don't know your name

I never saw your face

But I pray for peace

In your resting place

Bad Luck Glove

Your brittle dreams shatter like glass

Your hopes crumble into sand

And worry is the black velvet glove

That fits tight

On your bad luck hand

What's the Difference?

The difference isn't the colour

Of the individual threads

A rainbow formed from every hue

Of greens and blues and reds

The difference isn't the accents

Which give pattern and relief

Antipathy of monotone

Whatever your belief

The difference isn't the weave

The warp or the weft

By chance aligned north or south

Or woven right or left

The difference isn't the fibre

Wool or cotton or silk

Smooth to touch or coarse to last

Made from every ilk

The difference is the tapestry

The final finished whole

Uniquely bonded every strand

Each one an equal role

Black Kitten Heels

With your silver-tongued stories

And tin-plate tales

Fools-gold inventions

And mercurial intentions

Do you think I'm really taken in?

A snake cloaked in Versace

With a pet parrot called Archie

Who sits on your shoulder so fine

All high hopes and false fears

Through your party bathroom tears

You stand for nothing

In your black kitten heels

Yet you ask *me* how it feels

To be outside

And what do I think of the wine?

HMS Mutiny

This ship which to destruction sails

Is crewed and captained by alpha males

Judge and jury

Who make the rules

For those they take for ignorant fools

Actually, angels who fear to tread

But have no choice

For the rules dictate

They have no voice

Drugged and duped

And taken on board

By colluding press gangs

While the swinging corpse of justice

On the yardarm hangs

And so, we lumber on and on

To the tempestuous fury

Of a hurricane horizon

Through rough foam topped seas

These seasick sailors

Now down upon their knees

Immovable object

Meets irresistible force

Unable to change course

Because this ship is rigged

With a false design

A monstrous carbuncle

Built at the shipyard

That lined the pockets

Of the captain's uncle

Same deal

Same course

Same outcome

But I can only hope and pray

That I will wake one glorious day

And everyone will be with me

And we'll take the wheel

And rename this vessel

HMS Mutiny

Mirror in the Subway

Walking through the streets of London
Shops and galleries everywhere
Fancy dining bars and restaurants
Of Knightsbridge and Mayfair
I go down through the subway
To get to the other side
It's cold and dark and dirty
Not sure what it might hide
A man sleeps under cardboard
Another holds an empty cup
He's staring at the concrete
But as I pass, he looks up
His clothes are torn and ragged
He's old beyond his years
And as our eyes meet for a moment
I'm forced to face my fears
There's a mirror in the subway
You can choose what you see
Something that's not real
Or a picture of humanity
A meeting of the pathways
The destinies of life
A route to the subconscious
Crossroads of peace and strife

Some people's streets are lined with gold
Others are lined with gum
There's a mirror in the subway
You can either rest or run
But whether you choose to gaze ahead
Or stop to think or care
The reflection may seem transient
But it is always there
And as I climb back to the busy street
To resume my Sunday stroll
I muse on the mirror in the subway
And coins tossed in hope to save a soul

Graffiti

A chill wind courses through the subway
Litter scratches 'cross concrete floors
Hidden tales howl from the hollows
Striking slabs of angular graffiti
Masking grey municipal walls.
Penned by authors against authority
Coded symbols and covert signs
In a swordless counter-culture war
Fluorescent echoes, flickering glimpses

Frozen snapshots of daylight dreams
By hidden armies of lost souls
That speak of nineteen eighty-four.
Their colourful cries of freedom
Ring out like the bells of yore
Whilst the groaning ghosts of midnight
Prowl the fringes and shadows
Their tentacles of conformity
Lurk behind dark oppressive doors.

- - - - - - - - - - - - - - - - - - - -

Three Faces of the Antichrist

Walking in the heat of the valley of thieves
Brainwashed by serpents on the mount
We're being robbed of our humanity
A hold up that's history's greatest heist
Taken for fools to the fiery furnace
By three faces of the antichrist

Maybe stars, stripes, hammers or sickles
Pennies, roubles, cents or nickels
The roots of evil are now all rotten
Everything you touch is overpriced
Shepherds with cloven hooves run the farm
Amorphous form of the antichrist

It's twilight now on the ox and plough
Everything that moves is being rebranded
Food with less value than a soundbite
Sausage machine news so thinly sliced
Fat cats tossing scraps to the hamsters
Cunning cake crumbs of the antichrist

Democracy, autocracy, who really cares?
Masks and labels for the alpha
Persuade you to trade money for morals
Fall in line or be sacrificed
Innocent lambs slaughtered on the altar
Faustian contract of the antichrist

Power to the people was a mantra
A daydream shot dead in the back
Nothing really changed, it just got uglier
Dignity being dressed up and diced
Chefs with long knives in the Devil's kitchen
Assassins smile of the antichrist

666

Dr Martin Luther King

Stupid leaders

Stupid laws

Stupid guns

And stupid wars

The truth is *this*:

We haven't learned

A single useful thing

Since 6.05

On April 4th

'68

When the future died

Silenced by the gunshot

That slayed the giant

Dr Martin Luther King

Honesty

Where would we be

Without honesty?

She's not colourful

Or dressed in silk

Neither living loud

Nor peacock proud

Just taking care

And doing right

Through rainy days

And frosty nights

Working quietly

In the shade

For you and me

Where no-one busy

Looks to see

Her nestling in

The lower branches

Of society's redwood tree

- - - - - - - - - - - - - - - - - - -

The Waspish Sting of Truth

Sharp. Pointed. Singular. Compass needle

In a haystack of lies

Hides the waspish sting of truth

Echo

Counterfeit words
And conman hooks
A narcissist
Who always looks
Through gimlet eyes
And cheating teeth
For a fleeting chance
To catch a glance
In the shallow mere beneath
Or better still to linger upon
A vainglorious reflection
Of inner self
In every innocent living thing
In every freely given vista
In every phrase with hidden meaning
In the dusty books upon his shelf

Sleepwalk to Armageddon

Epochs, eras, and empires
Dynasties and domains
Past, present, and future
It's always been the same
Some new leader to fight for

Or perhaps a new religious cause
So, make hay whilst they reign
Because it starts and ends with wars
A clash of counter cultures
Meeting man to man head on
As you sleep walk to oblivion
On the road to Armageddon

Dictators and oligarchs
Authoritarian autocracies
Alpha addicts everywhere
Running the democracies
Designer suits and fake tan
PR'd hair, straight teeth, and set square jaws
Wallpaper covering the cracks
Because it starts and ends with wars
Election fair and election fraud
The pathways you were led on
They all seem to intersect
On the road to Armageddon

The strong keep getting stronger
The weak are leeched and sapped of power
Bucket brigades that transfer wealth
From mines to the ivory tower
Calloused hands that dig for gold
For the vaults of the rich to store

One day those hands will bear arms
Because it starts and ends with wars
Feasting at the all-day diner
You'll bite the hand you fed on
Equality was just a dream
On the road to Armageddon

Feuds for food and brawls for land
For water, oil and more
Conflict that might start at home
Or on a far-off foreign shore
Call it trade or piracy
Window dressed as international laws
Those windows are made of glass
Because it starts and ends with wars
Be careful of what you say
And whose toes you tread on
Be mindful of what you're thinking
On the road to Armageddon

Every day we're fighting fires
Flames fanned by the winds of greed
Heat rising in the kitchen
We'll burn the meals we need
Meantime the silicon chief
Whose rocket-fuelled phallus roars

Can't see wood from ashen trees
Because it starts and ends with wars
It's time now to get divorced
From the contract we were wed on
Highway of broken promises
On the road to Armageddon

Whatever happened to us
Sliding to a lazy demise
Sunset on this way of life
Look east for the new sunrise
Remember who you disrespect
Be it serfs or be it whores
The ladder always works both ways
Because it starts and ends with wars
So when you're looking down to
A bed you wouldn't be seen dead on
It's more comfortable than laying
On the road to Armageddon

So, over to you my children
This Gordian Knot yours to unpick
Bring back to balanced health
The earth that we made sick
Build a new house for all mankind
With solid roof and walls and floors
Please don't repeat our history

Because it starts and ends with wars
Discard the words and dogmas
Of lies you were born and bred on
And if you do you can step back
From the road to Armageddon

House of Hope

The house of hope is rotting
Time to seal up its roof and walls
Stop the rain of hate from creeping in
Before it crumbles and falls

Why?

Why are people hungry?
Why are they still cold?
Why are children dying?
With no hope of growing old?

Why more planes and warships?
Why more bullets and bombs?
Why worship possessions?
And not the things they're made from?

Why all the crooked leaders?
Why all the crooked smiles?
Why tilt the scales of justice?
To put truth not lies on trial?

Why accept the unequal?
Why not rage against the machine?
Why not rise and crush the system?
That's made us slaves to false dreams?

Power

The world is dangerous
And it seems it's getting more so by the hour
Everyday lives of everyday people
Hung out to dry by Neanderthals in power
A rise to the top where "More is more"
Money, guns and cocks
Let's round them up and put them to work
In a quarry breaking rocks

Warmongers

Warmongers have hijacked our religions
Turning words into guns and bombs
Mangling messages of love into hatred
Spreading a plague on x.com
The promise that's called the future
Is starting to get pretty small
In just one blink of the universe
I'll be come and I'll be gone
And soon mean nothing at all

- - - - - - - - - - - - - - - - - - - -

Time of Nights

It all seemed so perfect
Innocent, unbound and carefree
Picking fruit at will
From an ever-giving tree
But to everything there's a season
And the golden days of light
Are dimming fast as winter comes
It is the time of nights

- - - - - - - - - - - - - - - - - - - -

Conundrum

Don't know whether to respond or let go now
Don't want hear any more bad news
But if we don't fight for peace and justice
What else could we all stand to lose?
Angry world is making me angry
So many things to make you weep, oh Lord
Please don't let me become part of the problem
Trigger happy on a primed keyboard
I want a world where arms are for hugging
Hands held together or used to pray
Mouths for singing and lips for loving
Lessons we should've learned along the Baltic Way

End of Part 2

Part 3.

Black Dogs and White Cats

Storms of Rage

When your life's been gouged by tragedy
And you're stuck on the same page
May you find peace and tranquillity
To quell your storms of rage

Glimmer

Today I saw a glimmer
Of sunshine coming through
A single ray
Came streaming down
And I thought of you
I prayed that you might see it
To brighten up your day
To give you hope
That better times
Might be on their way

Giving

When your world has evaporated
When you're not sure how you can live
When everything has been taken
All you can do is give

- - - - - - - - - - - - - - - - - - -

So Much Undone

There's a time for everything
And for everything there's a time
But as the hourglass sifts sand
And the ticking clocks chime
I take stock of my achievements
Which count next to none
I feel life is slipping away
And there's so much still undone

- - - - - - - - - - - - - - - - - - -

One Day Nearer

Worried brow and troubled mind
Heavy heart, it's hard to find
A space where you can feel free
So, I'll try and help to make things clearer
By saying that you're one day nearer
To casting off your weighty shackles
And stepping lightly
Into the welcome world of liberty

- - - - - - - - - - - - - - - - - - -

Gem

How can one so beautiful
Have such pain inside
So kind and funny and caring
Until the day she died
On the outside so radiant
Inside a gemstone flawed
One day the gem just shattered
A million hopes upon the floor
And hope is all we have now
A hope you're not alone
A hope you're in a better place
A safer space that you call home

Laden

You're walking that same old road again
Your aching back is bent
The load you carry
Is racked and stacked
Full with memories
That nobody is allowed to see

But if I could help you carry it
Take the strain for just one dusty mile
Give your weary bones some respite
Let you feel the lightness of a smile
You know I surely would
I'd ask but you'd say don't
And you could always call me
But I know you won't
And so this is how it is
Time and distance grow
Burdens are the devils
We know and can't let go

Shell

You say you are no more than a shell
Hollowed out by heartbreak
Dissolved by despair
And the corrosion of loneliness
A void that used to be filled
With life and laughter and love

With warmth and comfort and joy
And though no-one's worthy to fill that space
Or be the flesh that gave you meaning
Come close for just a little while
Let me hold you softly in my arms
Rest quietly with me
And together we will listen
For in every shell there still resonates
A timeless record of everything
Wrapped up into a beautiful sound
That is the whisper of the sea

I'm a Tightrope Man

I'm a tightrope man
My head is on fire
Jelly legs are trembling
On a high tensile wire

First step's the hardest
Second's close behind
Uncertainty needs courage
It's all in the mind

Solid ground earth points
Connecting the chasm
Every nerve overloaded
My muscles in spasm

Down to the midpoint
Place of no return
The question of being
To crash or to burn

Sidewinds are blowing
Down the valley of fear
Everywhere you look
Nothing seems near

I can't help but wonder
What's the matter with me
The man that's inside
Ain't the man that you see

Deep breath and onwards
Up the gradual rise
Keep looking forward
I'm squinting my eyes

My feet sore from walking
My mind is deep fried
The canyon of insanity
Is a thousand miles wide

The closer you get
The more you can lose
The path that you're given
Isn't one that you choose

Fresh air beneath me
And above's looks just fine
Heaven and hell divided
By a thin steel line

Volcano

The heat inside is rising
The lava's beginning to flow
Seeping into fault lines
That come up from below
I'm anxious and wary
With only me to trust
Will the magma of subconscious
Rupture the fissures in the crust?
It's easy to get weary
It's easy to get tired
But I've got to keep on dousing flames
On my internal fire

Falling Off the Cliff

Every day the sun rises
Every day the sun sets
Same old story
Same old riff
How come if it's all so certain
Every day I feel like
I'm just one step
From falling off the cliff?

Valhalla Morn

Eyes glazed, I gazed out upon
My Valhalla morn
In pale monotone
Full moon lighting softly
Frozen ghosts in the icy white lake
Night's polarising scream
Wild peaks and deep troughs
Replaced by a heavy mood of gloom
A weight that breaks backs
Inertia and paralysis
Listless castaway adrift
At the water's border
The tree of life's branches

Jet black silhouettes
Hung in the scales of dawn
As if knowing what was at stake
Odin's presence loomed
Weary from battle
Resolve ebbing away
My shoulders bearing ravens
Of thought and memory
I stare down at the lake
Cold and lifeless
Promising to suck the warmth
From my tired body
Ready for my longboat journey
To take just one more step
To feel free at last
Unbound and liberated
Renewed and reborn
Redefined in the cosmos
But over the silent frost and snow
Huginn and Muninn gently whisper
Good things will still bloom
The aurora will be yours
And always, always
Glory will be in the battles won
And so, one thread of life is spun
I reach out with hesitant hand
I bide my time

Step back from the brink
A sharp sting of reality
Everything as before
Only now I am different
Wearing the invisible cloak
Of a nearly-being
Woven from the durable thread of shame
That will remain with me forever
Not a word to anyone
And the ghosts of the underworld
They must await another day
Unsettled and chattering
Like the teeth in my numb skull
And so life goes on
The cloak's weight becomes the norm
The days grow long again
And summers come
New flowers grow
Their eternal memory of rebirth
Gradually fills the void
And reclaims the barren wastelands
Colour returns and rivers flow
And slowly, slowly
Imperceptibly
Thought kindles desire
And desire kindles thought
I must return and see the other side

I must stand on the frozen lake
And look up, not down
To the black canvas universe
And wait and wait
Breathing in ice crystal air
Until at last
The great obsidian skies
Light up with faint trails
Hues of green and purple
Gradually enriching and revealing themselves
Dancing in mesmeric silence
Inky, slinky, shimmering ribbons
There for me
And they say "I told you,
I was here before
I will be here again
Sharing the mysteries
Visible to all open hearts and minds
That allow themselves to be
That believe there is a better day"

Crumbling

Why does every door handle

That promises so much

Crumble in my hands

And fall to the floor as dust?

Destroyer

Rays of sunshine

And rays of hope

I shut the blinds

And cut the rope

With every move

And at every turn

I smash my paths

And bridges burn

Will I ever stop

To look and see

The destroyer that lives

Inside of me?

Load

You need to see
You've got the world at your feet
And not on your shoulders
That problems are pebbles
Not great granite boulders
You need to feel that
You're swimming with the tide
Everything's possible
That luck's on your side
So, stop
Step back
Take time
Be reflective
Look for the good
And find your perspective

Kick the Can

And all I do is kick the tin can down the road
Keep thinking time will lighten my load
But what do I know?
Just how far have I got to go
Till I can rest easy in this skin of mine?

Yesterday

Yesterday it was all so clear
The feeling that ran in my blood
Now I'm cloaked in confusion fogs
And my mind's as clear as mud

But I can hope that tomorrow
This enveloping misty veil
Will burn away in the morning sun
And clarity once more prevail

Black Twin

I'm running as fast as I can
On and on
Towards the light
Not sure what I want to find
(Or maybe lose)
Down dark dead-ends lined
With false hopes
And peace signs
Hollow promises
And dissolving dreams
On and on
Towards the light
Squinting slits

Fixing my eyes on
A bleached horizon
And silhouette trees
Vague forms that rise from
The heat haze breeze
Time's in front of me
And time's behind
But you're never in either
Rooted in reality
That perpetual cusp
Everlasting transition
The here and now battlefield
Where the swords of hope and despair
Clash and clang
To record every blow
Every decision
That radiates and fades
Through the dissipating air
On and on
Towards the light
My hopeful heart's tiring
I'm nearly on my knees
Lungs fit to burst
Head swimming
But mouth dry
A dead man's thirst
The buzz of a fly

I glance over my shoulder
But my shadow's still close by
It's mine alone
Uninvited guest
Inseparable companion
From east to west
Mocking mimic
Silent spectre
A faceless form
Morphing, magnetic
Black blanket
Black partner
Black twin
Who disappears with the night
The enemy without
Now the enemy within
Seeping unnoticed
Inextricably entwined
In the voids and recesses
Of body and mind

This Too Shall Pass

On days like these you feel you're done
Every heartache rolled into one
The darkest clouds and driving rain
The agony of love expressed as pain
But to you I make this solemn vow
If you can accept the here and now
And likewise all that's gone before
This too shall pass
To a brighter place
Where torment and suffering will be no more

More is Less

The more I know
The less I learn
The more I look
The less I see
The more I climb
I fall further short
Of the man I want to be

Faded Rainbow

My rainbow colours
Once so vivid and well defined
Nailed firmly to the mast of hope
Have now run
Fuzzy and faded
From the myopic blur of time
Merging into one
Soft focus and ill defined
No longer wearing
The pride of innocence and naivety
But nonetheless
They're still here
Weathered but not beaten
By the winds of adversity
The winds of reality
The winds of experience
The winds of change
Shabby but not ashamed
They tell a unique story
Illuminated by many sunrises
The record of a journey
That whispers survival

Silent Witness

There's a sly eyed white feline

Who wears a black mask of death

With her soft padded paws

Wrapped up in satin and silk

She slipped into the room

About an hour ago

Unseen and unheard

Stretched out fully

On the fireside settle

Where the last embers glow

But a chill creeps in

She just waits and stares

But she doesn't stir

No purring or preening or licking

Just overseeing her duty

To the time lords of infinity

Who decide when and where

The clock of life will stop ticking

And once this simple task is complete

She slips down to the floor

Retraces her steps

Eyes forward, mono paced

Exits left by the door whence she came

Leaving without pity or prejudice

Another mortal soul

Who exhaled their last breath

And who's being is now your memory

No more thoughts

No more feelings

No more words to be spoken

All that was complex

Now vanished

Like the sly eyed white feline

Who bore silent witness

To this invisible line in the sand

Soul Unbound

You built your life on shifting sands

Toil and graft from your hard worked hands

Holes in the soles of your old leather shoes

No-one could say you haven't paid your dues

But you'll leave this world with your head held high

All chains unbound your soul will fly

To be with loved ones who've left these shores

Light and lightness evermore yours

Celestial Promise

If you ever worry

What the future holds

And whether you'll still be

Take comfort in the celestial promise

And rest assured

You were. You are. You will be.

End of Part 3.

Part 4.

Existence and Non-Existence

Summer

Haystack stubble fields of gold

Chalk streams flowing clear and cold

Watercress and abundant trout

Moorhen chicks, parents devout

Silhouette swifts on azure skies

Darting dashing dragonflies

Hedgerow blossoms turned to fruit

Goldfinches in gaudy suits

Past the solstice, daylight dimmer

But still the heated landscape shimmers

Rejoice and be glad for now at least

Indulge in summer's sensuous feast

Just a Second

Each brand-new second

Never been seen before

Rolls into my life

Through time's open door

Waiting in line

An endless chain

To be for one moment

Then never again

Touching both ends of eternity
Arm in arm, one by one
Marching faithful to the beat
Of infinity's drum
An abundance divisible
To a single moment of time
Containing more multitudes
Than I could ever put down in rhyme
But just imagine one second
Across the whole universe
Every particular action, reaction
In that instant so diverse
Every story of existence
Happening without seeing
Glorious, triumphant
The moment of being
Taken for granted
Like tides of the sea
What will I do with it?
What will it do with me?

Inferno

Raging fire-fuelled inferno flames
Flaring higher than Babel's tower
Holding us steady at arm's length
To give us heat and light and power

Ninety million miles away
No say, no wish, no fear
Was there ever a presence more true
Whom we should revere?

Rising up from the horizon line
Same place, same day each year
Giving life to every form
On this blue dependent sphere

A song of light that's joy to hear
Sung out each day before us
The dawn that puts night to bed
And wakes the morning chorus

And every leaf of every tree
Silent process of the seasons
From bud to coat of verdant green
Nature's rhyme and nature's reason

North and south take equal turns
To bow and show respect
Rewarded with another summer
And harvests to collect

Wise people of the ancient times
Hauled stones for pyramids and henges
To honour this celestial disc
That both anoints and avenges

Drawing water from the oceans
Inflating orbicular cloud trains
That stop to water temperate stations
With warm life-giving rains

Whilst concurrently in arid deserts
Relentless, searing heat
Powers an open death trap oven
That fries all that chance should meet

And me, I see light and shade
Feel warmth like a velvet gown
Take vitamin, strength and mood
And watch my skin turn brown

Apollo, Helios, Sol or Ra
Labels made as the ages churn
Yet before and after our own candle lives
Your constant heart will ever burn

Dear Universe

Thank you for the loan
Of these few atoms
That make me unique
May I be a good custodian
And use them wisely
Before they are given up
Once more to you
Unconditionally ad infinitum
To be used as you see fit

Plaintive Cry

And as I raise my head

From earth to sky

To seek the source

Of a plaintive cry

I see two brown buzzards

With wings spread wide

Seeking currents

On which to ride

Round and round

Unburdened, swift

Invisible thermal

Their souls to lift

Higher and higher

Looking down on me

Show the meaning

Of being free

Soft feather tips

Like fingers curl

To caress the wind

They fold and furl

And play the air

Like piano keys

Orchestrated

Above the listening trees

That hide and host

The twiggy nest

Where young have hatched

And safely rest

This ring of life

Simple, dependent

The natural rhythm

Of life resplendent

This Day

This day

This place

This moment

This walk

This forest

This hill top

This view

Is mine

And mine alone

Never happened before
Never happen again
This winter sun
This shaft of light
This long shadow
This dappled earth
This sapphire sky
This wispy cloud
This crisp silence
Is mine
And mine alone
Never happened before
Never happen again
This cool air
This breath in
This breath out
This fleeting thought
This tranquil peace
This boundless hunger
This life fulfilled
Is mine
And mine alone
Never happened before
Never happen again

Looking Back

One day when life's curtains
Are drawn across my road
I'll look back to the light
Where my river has flowed
And I hope it will shine
A thread that meanders
That offers some comfort
To the lonely bystander
Set in a landscape
Of each season's hues
No time for regrets
Or to pay more dues
What's been has been
It can't be undone
What's left on the easel
When the course is run
The judges will be quick
At the end of your race
As your colours radiate
Forever into space

Midnight Mayhem

Looking down at a colony of ants
Streams of headlights and taillights of cars
Up above moonlit trails from the planes
Join up the dots of the stars
Meanwhile on the busybody pavement
The weaving workers and the milling drones
Walk with heads bowed down in concentration
Staring at screens on their phones
And it all seems to work so perfectly
A carefully choreographed global play
This show can never pause and must go on
Dawn till dusk, night and day
But do you ever stop to wonder
What in the world can it possibly mean?
Maybe it means absolutely nothing
It's all just a wild crazy dream

Passing Through

I'm nothing special

Just water and dust

Come together by chance or design

Interim, short lived

Or makeshift if you must

A few tiny fragments

Universal matter

Bound pro tempore by time and place

Before breaking up

The four winds to scatter

And who knows what next?

What form and what shape?

Re-imagined and reinvented

Then stripped right back down

Once more to escape

Both hostage to fortune

Our paths destined to cross

I wonder at the purpose and forces

That placed us together

In God's great galactic chaos

Drifting though dark space
Since eternity's start
We've been here forever and ever
Let it be so
Till time's torn apart

Don't worry for me
Here from before you knew
And to be after all memories die
Entwined, always connected
We're just passing through

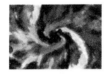

One Sun

It's the same sun that sets on the poor
That sets on the rich
It's the same sun that lights the path
That darkens the ditch
It's the same moon that rises for lovers
That rises for vampires
It's the same moon that waxes for the righteous
That wanes for liars

It's the same stars that shine for the living
That shine for the dead
It's the same stars that explode in fury
That live inside my head

- - - - - - - - - - - - - - - - - - -

Virus

Clever, conniving, cunning trickster
Driven to infect and thrive
To outlive and survive
Above all others
Allcomers that threaten to replace
Fight to flourish
Determined to dominate
But the really smart ones
Learn to coexist
Aware that killing the host
Is writing your own death warrant
Signed by your own hand
In your own blood
Only the stupid would do this
Much better not be too greedy
Adapt to respect your benefactor
And not provoke cataclysmic defences
But can we?

Will we?
Or are we the mad mutant
Hellbent on destroying
Our abundant keeper?

Ashes to Ashes

Ashes to ashes
Dust to dust
The world is on fire
We're bound and we're trussed

Ready to burn
On our own funeral pyre
That day after day
Gets hotter and higher

And in case you were hoping
For a reincarnation
No Phoenix will rise
From the mother of all cremations

Shifting Sands

This long and lonely path I've danced
On shifting, shoreline sands
Is met by lapping tongues of waves
Those packs of foaming hounds
That relentlessly advance
And without mercy will erase
Every step of hope that's walked
Each new beginning made
While ticking time's line quietly chalks
The receding quota of my days

Farm Lane Thriplow

These are the days
The spring sun slowly sinks
Trusty Helios driving his chariot
Towards oblivion for you and I
Whilst simultaneously
Casting a soft ochreous light
That lifts the mist
And lights the sky
In some far-off foreign land.

Meanwhile, in Thriplow village fair
The daffodil banks along Farm Lane
A golden orchestra of trumpets
With stand-to-attention fresh green stems
Fight for their moment of glory
Before retreating for another year
Recovered in a darkened earthy womb
Then bursting forth once more
Springtime's guard of honour
Lining the winding way
Of this ancient avenue
Whose surface acts as impromptu canvas
For the dancing dappled shadows
Brushed in subtle shades
As the day's last rays
From the sinking orange orb
Thread their warming way
Between the expectant, grateful
Gently swaying twigs and boughs
A perfect scene of the here and now

Longing

One foot on the shore
The other in the sea
Each one forever wishing
To walk where the other would be

- - - - - - - - - - - - - - - - - - -

Time Lapse

As I sat in the forest
And slowly breathed still air
In one musing moment
I departed my earthly body
Tethered to the ground
Bound by leathery straps
And so, I rose up to see
My own life beneath
From a heaven-kissed canopy.
With amusement and pity
I looked down upon
The briefest flicker
Just one frame in a film
An epic time lapse sequence
Projected onto a vast silver screen
That stretched up and out forever
Across the deep indigo skies

With a symphonic soundtrack
And me second fiddle
All haste and hurry
Burning bright as I could
Before darkness descends
And silence transcends
Both the great and the good.

But as I thought more
Just maybe, perhaps
I have no beginning
And I have no end
I've been here forever
Because *I* am infinity
Both prologue and epilogue
I am the glittering first dust
And I am the dark in the void
After the last stars collapse.

- - - - - - - - - - - - - - - - - - - -

Journeyman

I'm really just a journeyman
A travelling man passing through
Forgotten places and forgotten faces
Forgotten by everyone I ever knew

- - - - - - - - - - - - - - - - - - - -

The Orchard Cabin

The orchard cabin

With rounded roof

And welcoming windows

Stands solid on four cast iron wheels

A shepherd's hut so called

Cosy haven of tranquillity

Nestled amongst fruit laden trees

Gorgeous apples, pears and plums

Soaking up the summer sun

To swell, sweeten and soften ready to pick

Whilst heaven scented lavender bushes

Pastel stems and plump purple flowers

Reaching up and joyously reverberating

With the strains of the working bees

Whose labour will turn to liquescent heaven

In honeycombed hives just a mile away

And the lush green grass sward

Feeds the soft dark brown fleeces

Of the hard horned Hebridean sheep

Laconically meandering and munching

In contrast to the skittish bobbing rabbits

And the busy tapping woodpecker

Black and white with a flash of red

Disturbing my afternoon reverie

And as I open my eyes and look to the skies
I see fast and furious swallows
Taking invisible sustenance in thin air
Whilst a buzzard glides and mews
Looking for some larger unsuspecting morsel far below
And these same skies will later fall silent
Darkening to reveal a million stars and galaxies
All shining spectacularly sharp
Save for the milky band which defines the edges
Of our own lonely spiral
And I will still sit outside
With hazel log embers hissing and spitting
To keep my body and soul warm
And I'll look up to the majestic black canopy
Grateful for all I have witnessed this day

Cornish Dreams

Up and down the Cornish lanes
Not straight, but narrow
With grassy middles
And high banks of layered slate and grey granite
A hard core hidden by a soft deceptive sheath

Ferns and foxgloves

Bright buddleias and campions

Silent sirens to the bees and butterflies

An armada of red admirals, peacocks, gatekeepers

Burnets and browns

Purposeful players

With instinctive and intricate roles

In a finely balanced ad hoc play

That performs for us by moon or sun

And I walk and walk like bygone days

These same lanes and paths and byways

Frequented by the journeymen, the wool gatherers, the balers

Heathens and holy men

Simple folk and scholars

Medicine men and mothers

Minstrels and masons

Teachers and trussers

Lawyers and lovers

All treated evenly

By the undulating way

Beyond whose fringes

The heath opens up

Stunted trees with wind set branches

Hardy heathers

Fighting for attention with the prickly gaudy gorse

And yet more ferns, green with rusty fringes

Hinting at what's to come

As the summer solstice

Slips into the recesses of memory

And terra firma finishes

Arrested and imprisoned at the cliff's edge

Abrupt barrier that lets nothing past

Unless of course it has wings

Feathered fans of freedom

To come and go as you please

Gliding effortlessly on invisible drafts

That veer up the vertical stacks

Unbound by laws of gravity

Surveying the solid rocks below

Which in turn are washed and scrubbed

By the foaming salted seas

Arriving wave after wave from some far-off place

Hungry to devour the living earth

One grain at a time

To reclaim that which once was theirs

And I walk and watch and wonder

What is my place in this perfect, sacred scene?

Mountain Bound

I need to get back on the trail
A cure I know that never fails
And whenever I venture there
I renew my lungs with mountain air
Lose my breath on the rocky rise
Cut loose all weighty urban ties
Smell the scent of the steadfast pines
Find myself and my sense of time
Footfalls cushioned on the forest floor
Among the crags and peaks of Durmitor
Or maybe every now and then
In the heathered carpets of Scottish glens
Or under a blanket of stars at night
On some high plateau in the Dolomites
But wherever the path may take me
I know it will always make me
Fill my heart with hope and grace
Feel alive and know my place

Ticket Inspector

The night train slowly chunters on
The sonorous rails are humming
All aboard are sleeping soundly
But the ticket inspector's coming
To check your fare is valid
And you've made your declaration
Paid your debts and the ferryman
To that longed-for destination
Alighting at the pearly platform
That leads to the celebration
Fill your lungs and sing your heart out
In the celestial congregation

- - - - - - - - - - - - - - - - - - - -

Now

I am the mercurial conduit
Gatekeeper of all things future and past
I am indivisibly present in all that you are
Inextricably bound in both your memory and musing
I am the magician that tricks you into thinking you're real
Because there is no future or past, only now
But there is no now, because what was yet to be
Has, in one infinitely small instant, gone!
I am the joker called time

Runaway Train

The engine's getting louder
And it's picking up more speed
We're all aboard a runaway train
In pursuit of growth and greed
Fuelled by a burning desire
To have more than you need

We're far too busy working
To properly think things through
And anyway no-one knows
Exactly what to do
To change the train's direction
And go to someplace new

It all seemed so laudable
This materialistic dream
Building up momentum
Since the age of steam
To bring comforts to our lives
In a complex pyramid scheme

But to keep the fires burning
On this great insatiable beast
Needed new fuel and lubricant
To keep the wheels greased
So we farmed out our factory jobs
To cheap labour in the east

Sure enough as the saying goes
You reap just what you sow
The new empires awakened
And they too wanted to grow
Created in our own likeness
Yet helpless to say no

A self-fulfilling system
Where no solution has been found
Kidding ourselves it'll all work out
That there's enough to go around
As train hurtles to a cliff edge
Where everyone is drowned

So come on everybody
Let's cool this huff and puff
Start building our wellbeing
Instead of junk and stuff
To understand what's good for us
And know when enough's enough

Liquid Pearl

All that I need
To re-balance and renew
Is to see the tip of a single verdant blade of grass
Bend and glisten in the rising sun
Before shedding its transient weight
Giving birth to
A shimmering bulbous made-for-me
Liquid pearl of dew

End of Part 4

Also by John Deed:

Elemental Poems
Of Being. Of the Mind. Of the Heart

First published in 2021, this is John's first collection of poems, exploring three important themes in our existence. They are a very personal view, but hopefully very accessible to those of an inquisitive nature.

The A to Z of Country Limericks

A light-hearted collection of nonsense rhymes published in 2020, with vibrant and engaging cartoon illustrations by Sean MacGarry, suitable for children aged 5 to100!

One country is covered for each letter of the alphabet (including a little poetic licence when we get to "X"!). These limericks primarily aim to amuse, but with an additional sprinkling of interesting facts about each country "visited", they might also stimulate the enquiring mind.

Both books are available as softback or Kindle

Find out more at:
flyingpigments.co.uk

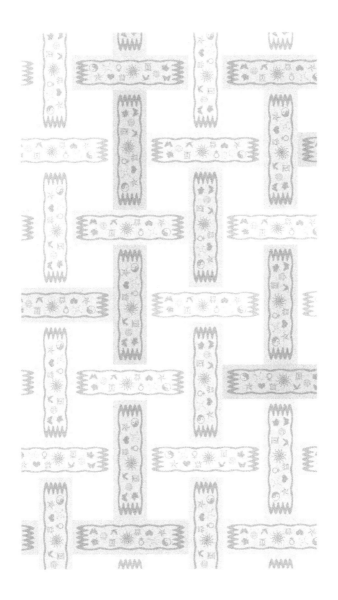

137

Printed in Great Britain
by Amazon

49172138R00088